Meeting God in the Flesh

8 Discussions for the Curious and Skeptical

Don Everts

InterVarsity Press
Downers Grove, Illinois

InterVarsity Press
P.O. Box 1400, Downers Grove, IL 60515-1426
World Wide Web: www.ivpress.com
E-mail: mail@ivpress.com

InterVarsity Press® is the book-publishing division of InterVarsity Christian Fellowship/USA®, a student movement active on campus at hundreds of universities, colleges and schools of nursing in the United States of America, and a member movement of the International Fellowship of Evangelical Students. For information about local and regional activities, write Public Relations Dept., InterVarsity Christian Fellowship/USA, 6400 Schroeder Rd., P.O. Box 7895, Madison, WI 53707-7895, or visit the IVCF website at <www.intervarsity.org>.

Design: Matt Smith
Images: Creatas

ISBN 0-8308-2089-2

Printed in the United States of America ∞

P	18	17	16	15	14	13	12	11	10	9	8	7	6	5	4	3	2	1
Y	18	17	16	15	14	13	12	11	10	09	08	07	06	05					

Contents

Introduction

What Would It Have Been Like to Meet Jesus?

Jesus of Nazareth: a man who lived two thousand years ago. A seemingly simple man who spent most of his life as a carpenter. Probably a strong man, given his profession. But strong arms alone cannot explain how a simple man who never traveled far from home became such a looming figure in world history.

After two thousand years, his name is known almost everywhere. His teachings have been copied, memorized and adored throughout the centuries. Two simple lines (in the form of a cross) remind everyone of the epic ending of his life. It's a famous story. And famously debated.

All from this one man.

But when you brush aside all the centuries of loud worship and debate and controversy, you may just wonder what he was really like. As a man.

What would it have been like to meet him? How would he have acted? What was his manner among men and women . . . and kids? How would I have reacted to him? Would I like sitting with him? Would I be interested in what he had to say?

A CHAPTER IN THE LIFE OF JESUS

If these questions intrigue you as much as they intrigue me, you'll be pleased to know that the events of Jesus' life were recorded. He had such an impact on people (even in his own day) that several people felt called to write down the story of his life. These books were called "Gospels"—a word borrowed from Jesus' teaching.

The most ancient of these books is called "The Gospel According to Mark" (or just "Mark"). Mark is an ancient Greek book, probably written around A.D. 65, and is the shortest Gospel by far. It's about the size of a short story.

The Mark text is written in rough, unsophisticated Greek. It's a straightforward story of Jesus' life, short and to the point most of the time. But at certain points its pages slow down and offer some enlightening personal details about this man Jesus.

Most scholars agree that this ancient text was written by a fellow named John Mark. John Mark was a good friend of Simon Peter, who was one of the closest friends Jesus ever had. There are so many personal, detailed descriptions of Jesus in this little biography that it is concluded by most scholars that John Mark was writing down the life of Jesus as told to him by Simon Peter.

If you are curious about what it would have been like to meet Jesus, you could read Mark. Even just one chapter of Mark shows us Jesus in detail, living out his life among people. How did those people like him? How did they react to him? What did they do together? Mark is a great place to start to look for answers to these questions.

I figured the first chapter of Mark is as good a place to start as any, so I went ahead and wrote this discussion guide around Mark 1.

EIGHT DISCUSSIONS

Luckily, folks have already translated Mark 1 from ancient Greek into English. That was helpful. But there's still some historical and cultural stuff involved that needs to be learned about and thought through. So I broke the first chapter of Mark up into eight bite-sized sections to make it more manageable.

Taking the time to really "enter into" each section of Mark 1 by learning about culturally relevant facts and asking questions to get at the real meat of the story is important. So I've got four separate exercises to help us not just passively read but really actively read the eight sections of the text.

These four exercises should help us better answer our questions about Jesus—and they may make the process more fun.

1. JESUS UNDER A MICROSCOPE

We begin by focusing. To do this exercise, it's important to get tunnel vision and so focus in on the text that we forget about everything in our peripheral vision.

We'll eventually pull our heads away from the "microscope," but first we have to take the text seriously. It's an important document and a great source for information on what Jesus was really like. So we will begin by reading in depth a small section from Mark 1.

I think one of the biggest mistakes in talking about Jesus is to stay aloof from him and talk in generalities and stereotypes. It may serve us to grab this one chapter and study it perhaps more deeply than we've ever studied one chapter before.

So we begin by reading the actual text. (Well, an English translation of it.) I recommend taking a pen and maybe some highlighters and really getting involved with the verses.

I love reading, but I simply can't read without a pen in my hand anymore. I underline things that seem important, put marks next to words that get repeated a couple of times, draw smiley faces next to words or phrases or thoughts I like, put huge question marks next to things that don't make sense.

With old texts like Mark (which in Greek don't have any paragraph breaks), I look for different "thought chunks" and make paragraph separations. Stuff like that.

The reason I do this is because it keeps me from just reading words on a page. It helps me get involved with the ideas and thoughts and images and story elements that are there. I recommend this approach highly. Especially when we're dealing with an ancient text like this, there's got to be some work involved to get to the true story of the text—and ultimately the man Jesus.

So start by reading the text a few times and marking it up with your pen and highlighters.

Then walk through some of the comments and questions I've provided. If you're with other folks, you can discuss these questions together. These questions are just suggested places to start in thinking through and discussing the text. I only included ones I thought could be helpful, but I am not assuming all of them will be for you. So just use the ones that help you see the text more clearly.

2. JESUS THROUGH A TELESCOPE

If the first exercise is putting the text under a microscope, this second exercise is more like using a telescope. You see, Mark 1 will be most helpful in answering our questions about Jesus if it shows us stuff about him that was really true and typical of what he was like most of the time. One of the ways to check for that being the case is to pull our heads away from the microscope and consider what we find in the rest of Mark and what other Gospel writers wrote about Jesus.

So I went ahead and gathered together some verses from other places that we can fast-forward through to get a broader scope on Jesus. I mostly stuck with verses that show the people around Jesus responding to him. I figured that's a great place to start for insights on what it would be like to meet Jesus—by looking at those who really did!

Go ahead and read through all of these verses (remember how helpful a pen or highlighter can be) and look for connections between them and what we saw in the Mark 1 text. Hopefully this will not only confirm some of what we saw about Jesus in Mark but will also nuance and clarify our understanding of him.

Think of it as a way of going back over a simple pencil drawing of Jesus and adding more detail and erasing extraneous lines. Taking into account more verses about Jesus will hopefully result in a much clearer, more accurate view of him as a man.

3. WHAT KIND OF JESUS?

If we take both an in-depth look at Jesus through a microscope and a broad look at Jesus through a telescope, we'll likely end up with some great clarity about what he was really like.

This third (and potentially final) exercise is a chance to ask some deeper questions about how the long list of verses relates to the section we studied in Mark. I've included some discussion questions that may help us come to some conclusions about what Jesus was really like.

There will also be a couple of questions that help us interact with Jesus as well as some of my own thoughts about these images of Jesus that I put in my book *God in the Flesh*. Lately I've been asking lots of questions about Jesus and how people responded to him in his own day. I thought that some of my ideas might add juice to your own conversations and thoughts.

4. FURTHER EXPERIMENTS

This fourth exercise is totally optional. If you find yourself wanting to study more or think more or experience more about the image of Jesus that has come out of the section in Mark, I provided some ways to do that.

Read through the options, if you want, and see whether one sticks out to you. Depending on what questions are still lingering with you after reading the Mark text, you might find a "further experiment" that fits you. If you're having these discussions in a group, there may be one you'd want to do together.

I do hope you enjoy this chapter in the life of Jesus. And mostly I hope that we all see this intriguing man a little more clearly. That we have more of a sense of what it would have been like to meet the man who has created so much of a fuss the world over.

Maybe we'll have a better sense of what the fuss is all about.

1 ¹αρξη του ευαγγελιου ιησου χριστου [υιου θεου]. ²καθως γεγραπται εν τω ησαια τω προφητη, ιδου αποστελλω τον αγγελον μου προ προσωπου σου, ος κατασκευασει την οδον σου: ³φωνη βοωντος εν τη ερημω, ετοιμασατε την οδον κυριου, ευθειας ποιειτε τας τριβους αυτου ⁴εγενετο ιωαννης [ο] βαπτιζων εν τη ερημω και κηρυσσων βαπτισμα μετανοιας εις αφεσιν αμαρτιων. ⁵και εξεπορευετο προς αυτον πασα η ιουδαια χωρα και οι ιεροσολυμιται παντες, και εβαπτιζοντο υπ αυτου εν τω ιορδανη ποταμω εξομολογουμενοι τας αμαρτιας αυτων. ⁶και ην ο ιωαννης ενδεδυμενος τριχας καμηλου και ζωνην δερματινην περι την οσφυν αυτου, και εσθιων ακριδας και μελι αγριον. ⁷και εκηρυσσεν λεγων, ερχεται ο ισχυροτερος μου οπισω μου, ου ουκ ειμι ικανος κυψας λυσαι τον ιμαντα των υποδηματων αυτου: ⁸εγω εβαπτισα υμας υδατι, αυτος δε βαπτισει υμας εν πνευματι αγιω. ⁹και εγενετο εν εκειναις ταις ημεραις ηλθεν ιησους απο ναζαρετ της γαλιλαιας και εβαπτισθη εις τον ιορδανην υπο ιωαννου. ¹⁰και ευθυς αναβαινων εκ του υδατος ειδεν σχιζομενους τους ουρανους και το πνευμα ως περιστεραν καταβαινον εις αυτον: ¹¹και φωνη εγενετο εκ των ουρανων, συ ει ο υιος μου ο αγαπητος, εν σοι ευδοκησα. **2** ¹²και ευθυς το πνευμα αυτον εκβαλλει εις την ερημον. ¹³και ην εν τη ερημω τεσσερακοντα ημερας πειραζομενος υπο του σατανα, και ην μετα των θηριων, και οι αγγελοι διηκονουν αυτω. ¹⁴μετα δε το παραδοθηναι τον ιωαννην ηλθεν ο ιησους εις την γαλιλαιαν κηρυσσων το ευαγγελιον του θεου ¹⁵και λεγων οτι πεπληρωται ο καιρος και ηγγικεν η βασιλεια του θεου: μετανοειτε και πιστευετε εν τω ευαγγελιω. **3** ¹⁶και παραγων παρα την θαλασσαν της γαλιλαιας ειδεν σιμωνα και ανδρεαν τον αδελφον σιμωνος αμφιβαλλοντας εν τη θαλασση: ησαν γαρ αλιεις. ¹⁷και ειπεν αυτοις ο ιησους, δευτε οπισω μου, και ποιησω υμας γενεσθαι αλιεις ανθρωπων. ¹⁸και ευθυς αφεντες τα δικτυα ηκολουθησαν αυτω. ¹⁹και προβας ολιγον ειδεν ιακωβον τον του ζεβεδαιου και ιωαννην τον αδελφον αυτου, και αυτους εν τω πλοιω καταρτιζοντας τα δικτυα, **4** ²⁰και ευθυς εκαλεσεν αυτους. και αφεντες τον πατερα αυτων ζεβεδαιον εν τω πλοιω μετα των μισθωτων απηλθον οπισω αυτου. ²¹και εισπορευονται εις καφαρναουμ. και ευθυς τοις σαββασιν εισελθων εις την συναγωγην εδιδασκεν. ²²και εξεπλησσοντο επι τη διδαχη αυτου, ην γαρ διδασκων αυτους ως εξουσιαν εχων και ουχ ως οι γραμματεις. **5** ²³και ευθυς ην εν τη συναγωγη αυτων ανθρωπος εν πνευματι ακαθαρτω, και ανεκραξεν ²⁴λεγων, τι ημιν και σοι, ιησου ναζαρηνε; ηλθες απολεσαι ημας; οιδα σε τις ει, ο αγιος του θεου. ²⁵και επετιμησεν αυτω ο ιησους λεγων, φιμωθητι και εξελθε εξ αυτου. ²⁶και σπαραξαν αυτον το πνευμα το ακαθαρτον και φωνησαν φωνη μεγαλη εξηλθεν εξ αυτου. ²⁷και εθαμβηθησαν απαντες, ωστε συζητειν προς εαυτους λεγοντας, τι εστιν τουτο; διδαχη καινη κατ εξουσιαν: και τοις πνευμασι τοις ακαθαρτοις επιτασσει, και υπακουουσιν αυτω. ²⁸και εξηλθεν η ακοη αυτου ευθυς πανταχου εις ολην την περιχωρον της γαλιλαιας. **6** ²⁹και ευθυς εκ της συναγωγης εξελθοντες ηλθον εις την οικιαν σιμωνος και ανδρεου μετα ιακωβου και ιωαννου. ³⁰η δε πενθερα σιμωνος κατεκειτο πυρεσσουσα, και ευθυς λεγουσιν αυτω περι αυτης. ³¹και προσελθων ηγειρεν αυτην κρατησας της χειρος: και αφηκεν αυτην ο πυρετος, και διηκονει αυτοις. ³²οψιας δε γενομενης, οτε εδυ ο ηλιος, εφερον προς αυτον παντας τους κακως εχοντας και τους δαιμονιζομενους: ³³και ην ολη η πολις επισυνηγμενη προς την θυραν. ³⁴και εθεραπευσεν πολλους κακως εχοντας ποικιλαις νοσοις, και δαιμονια πολλα εξεβαλεν, και ουκ ηφιεν λαλειν τα δαιμονια, οτι ηδεισαν αυτον. **7** ³⁵και πρωι εννυχα λιαν αναστας εξηλθεν και απηλθεν εις ερημον τοπον κακει προσηυχετο. ³⁶και κατεδιωξεν αυτον σιμων και οι μετ αυτου, ³⁷και ευρον αυτον και λεγουσιν αυτω οτι παντες ζητουσιν σε. ³⁸και λεγει αυτοις, αγωμεν αλλαχου εις τας εχομενας κωμοπολεις, ινα και εκει κηρυξω: εις τουτο γαρ εξηλθον. ³⁹και ηλθεν κηρυσσων εις τας συναγωγας αυτων εις ολην την γαλιλαιαν και τα δαιμονια εκβαλλων. **8** ⁴⁰και ερχεται προς αυτον λεπρος παρακαλων αυτον [και γονυπετων] και λεγων αυτω οτι εαν θελης δυνασαι με καθαρισαι. ⁴¹και σπλαγχνισθεις εκτεινας την χειρα αυτου ηψατο και λεγει αυτω, θελω, καθαρισθητι: ⁴²και ευθυς απηλθεν απ αυτου η λεπρα, και εκαθαρισθη. ⁴³και εμβριμησαμενος αυτω ευθυς εξεβαλεν αυτον, ⁴⁴και λεγει αυτω, ορα μηδενι μηδεν ειπης, αλλα υπαγε σεαυτον δειξον τω ιερει και προσενεγκε περι του καθαρισμου σου α προσεταξεν μωυσης, εις μαρτυριον αυτοις. ⁴⁵ο δε εξελθων ηρξατο κηρυσσειν πολλα και διαφημιζειν τον λογον, ωστε μηκετι αυτον δυνασθαι φανερως εις πολιν εισελθειν, αλλ εξω επ ερημοις τοποις ην: και ηρχοντο προς αυτον παντοθεν.

1 [1] The beginning of the gospel about Jesus Christ, the Son of God. [2] It is written in Isaiah the prophet: "I will send my messenger ahead of you, who will prepare your way"—[3] "a voice of one calling in the desert, 'Prepare the way for the Lord, make straight paths for him.'" [4] And so John came, baptizing in the desert region and preaching a baptism of repentance for the forgiveness of sins. [5] The whole Judean countryside and all the people of Jerusalem went out to him. Confessing their sins, they were baptized by him in the Jordan River. [6] John wore clothing made of camel's hair, with a leather belt around his waist, and he ate locusts and wild honey. [7] And this was his message: "After me will come one more powerful than I, the thongs of whose sandals I am not worthy to stoop down and untie. [8] I baptize you with water, but he will baptize you with the Holy Spirit." [9] At that time Jesus came from Nazareth in Galilee and was baptized by John in the Jordan. [10] As Jesus was coming up out of the water, he saw heaven being torn open and the Spirit descending on him like a dove. [11] And a voice came from heaven: "You are my Son, whom I love; with you I am well pleased."

2 [12] At once the Spirit sent him out into the desert, [13] and he was in the desert forty days, being tempted by Satan. He was with the wild animals, and angels attended him. [14] After John was put in prison, Jesus went into Galilee, proclaiming the good news of God. [15] "The time has come," he said. "The kingdom of God is near. Repent and believe the good news!"

3 [16] As Jesus walked beside the Sea of Galilee, he saw Simon and his brother Andrew casting a net into the lake, for they were fishermen. [17] "Come, follow me," Jesus said, "and I will make you fishers of men." [18] At once they left their nets and followed him. [19] When he had gone a little farther, he saw James son of Zebedee and his brother John in a boat, preparing their nets. **4** [20] Without delay he called them, and they left their father Zebedee in the boat with the hired men and followed him. [21] They went to Capernaum, and when the Sabbath came, Jesus went into the synagogue and began to teach. [22] The people were amazed at his teaching, because he taught them as one who had authority, not as the teachers of the law.

5 [23] Just then a man in their synagogue who was possessed by an evil spirit cried out, [24] "What do you want with us, Jesus of Nazareth? Have you come to destroy us? I know who you are—the Holy One of God!" [25] "Be quiet!" said Jesus sternly. "Come out of him!" [26] The evil spirit shook the man violently and came out of him with a shriek. [27] The people were all so amazed that they asked each other, "What is this? A new teaching—and with authority! He even gives orders to evil spirits and they obey him." [28] News about him spread quickly over the whole region of Galilee. **6** [29] As soon as they left the synagogue, they went with James and John to the home of Simon and Andrew. [30] Simon's mother-in-law was in bed with a fever, and they told Jesus about her. [31] So he went to her, took her hand and helped her up. The fever left her and she began to wait on them. [32] That evening after sunset the people brought to Jesus all the sick and demon-possessed. [33] The whole town gathered at the door, [34] and Jesus healed many who had various diseases. He also drove out many demons, but he would not let the demons speak because they knew who he was. **7** [35] Very early in the morning, while it was still dark, Jesus got up, left the house and went off to a solitary place, where he prayed. [36] Simon and his companions went to look for him, [37] and when they found him, they exclaimed: "Everyone is looking for you!" [38] Jesus replied, "Let us go somewhere else—to the nearby villages—so I can preach there also. That is why I have come." [39] So he traveled throughout Galilee, preaching in their synagogues and driving out demons. **8** [40] A man with leprosy came to him and begged him on his knees, "If you are willing, you can make me clean." [41] Filled with compassion, Jesus reached out his hand and touched the man. "I am willing," he said. "Be clean!" [42] Immediately the leprosy left him and he was cured. [43] Jesus sent him away at once with a strong warning: [44] "See that you don't tell this to anyone. But go, show yourself to the priest and offer the sacrifices that Moses commanded for your cleansing, as a testimony to them." [45] Instead he went out and began to talk freely, spreading the news. As a result, Jesus could no longer enter a town openly but stayed outside in lonely places. Yet the people still came to him from everywhere.

²As it is written in the prophet Isaiah,

> "See, I am sending my messenger ahead of you,
>> who will prepare your way;
> ³the voice of one crying out in the wilderness:
>> 'Prepare the way of the Lord,
>> make his paths straight,' "

⁴John the baptizer appeared in the wilderness, proclaiming a baptism of repentance for the forgiveness of sins. ⁵And people from the whole Judean countryside and all the people of Jerusalem were going out to him, and were baptized by him in the river Jordan, confessing their sins. ⁶Now John was clothed with camel's hair, with a leather belt around his waist, and he ate locusts and wild honey. ⁷He proclaimed, "The one who is more powerful than I is coming after me; I am not worthy to stoop down and untie the thong of his sandals. ⁸I have baptized you with water; but he will baptize you with the Holy Spirit."

⁹In those days Jesus came from Nazareth of Galilee and was baptized by John in the Jordan. ¹⁰And just as he was coming up out of the water, he saw the heavens torn apart and the Spirit descending like a dove on him. ¹¹And a voice came from heaven, "You are my Son, the Beloved; with you I am well pleased."

Verse 1
The first sentence isn't really a sentence. It is probably what the author of the book intended to be its title. How do you like it as a title? What does the title communicate and make clear?

Verses 2-3
What does the prophecy tell us about the "messenger"? What's

the messenger's purpose? What do you think it means to make "straight paths"?

Verses 4-6

If you were a filmmaker, how would you film this wilderness baptism scene? Who would you get to play John?

What's the connection between the prophecy about a messenger and the story of John?

How does mass public confession "prepare the way" for the Messiah? What does that imply about the coming of the Messiah?

Verses 7-8

So, what's John teaching out there in the wilderness? What different questions might the crowds have after confessing their sins and then hearing this message?

Verses 9-11

What are the differences between the description of Jesus' baptism and the baptisms described in verse 5?

Overview

Given the title of this book, why do you think Mark begins with these opening scenes? What's the overall message of this opening section?

JESUS THROUGH A TELESCOPE

It isn't only in these eleven verses that we encounter people who think Jesus is extraordinary. Wherever Jesus goes, people find themselves responding to his divine nature. It's like a chorus of worship follows him wherever he goes.

Let's pull back from the text in Mark and consider a panorama of verses.

Those in the boat worshiped him, saying, "Truly you are the Son of God." (Matthew 14:33)

They came to him, took hold of his feet, and worshiped him. (Matthew 28:9)

When they saw him, they worshiped him. (Matthew 28:17)

They worshiped him, and returned to Jerusalem with great joy; and they were continually in the temple blessing God. (Luke 24:52-53)

He said, "Lord, I believe." And he worshiped him. (John 9:38)

Fear seized all of them; and they glorified God. (Luke 7:16)

Amazement seized all of them, and they glorified God. (Luke 5:26)

When he laid his hands on her, immediately she stood up straight and began praising God. (Luke 13:13)

Immediately he regained his sight and followed him, glorifying God; and all the people, when they saw it, praised God. (Luke 18:43)

The whole multitude of the disciples began to praise God joyfully with a loud voice. (Luke 19:37)

When the centurion saw what had taken place, he praised God. (Luke 23:47)

DIVINE JESUS?

What are some similarities among these verses? Differences?

What are some possible reasons why people responded to Jesus in these ways?

Read the following quote and then discuss the questions that follow it.

> Now, I am assuming that having church on the street corner, by yourself, was as awkward back then as I can imagine it being today. Especially if it was another person that you were worshiping. Especially if it was some blue-collar worker dressed like everyone else, or perhaps more poorly than everyone else, that you were worshiping. . . .
>
> Jesus' divinity, his Godness, struck many he came into contact with. And they just up and worshiped. This response is recorded throughout the Gospels. And we never see any folded bulletins or Sunday-go-to-meeting clothes or organs to get them in the mood. They just praised God. Joyfully.
>
> This was a chance for pure worship, after all: no in-between priests, no hierarchical temple structure, no need to wrack the brain to remember the good deeds of God. No. He was right there in front of them.
>
> God was near and touchable.
>
> But streets were not the appropriate place to worship in those days. And dusty carpenters have never been the right object of worship. So these impromptu outbursts must have caused quite a commotion.
>
> —from chapter four, "They Worshiped Him," in *God in the Flesh*

What strikes you from this quote? What do you agree or disagree with?

What do you think it was like for the crowds when someone came and grabbed Jesus' feet and worshiped him?

On an average day, what would it take for you to worship someone—or to start worshiping God because of someone?

In the end, why do you think the authors of the four Gospels bothered to record these verses describing folks worshiping Jesus?

FURTHER EXPERIMENTS IN WORSHIP

- Study Mark 11:1-10, where we see whole crowds of people proclaiming Jesus' true nature. Why do you think Jesus' last entry into Jerusalem happened this way? How do you reconcile this story with the fact that crowds in Jerusalem would yell for Jesus' death only days later?

- Read chapter four, "They Worshiped Him," in *God in the Flesh*.

- Find a friend who goes to a Christian church and ask if you can tag along to watch the people worshiping Jesus. Just sit back and observe. What do you notice? What do you feel? What questions do you have? If you feel comfortable, ask one or two of the folks afterward what it is like to worship Jesus and why they do it.

- The Psalms is a book in the Hebrew Scriptures (the Christian "Old Testament") that is filled with worship poems and songs. Try reading through some of them and see what you notice. Does anything surprise you?

2

They Struck His Head

In this session we're taking a stroll on the dark side of the Gospels. You see, it turns out that not everyone responded to Jesus by worshiping him. Some people hated him. Yeah, hated. Lots of folks wanted to kill him, throw him off a cliff, whatever it took. It's a pretty strong reaction to have to someone.

Are there many people you've really hated during your life? Have you ever hated some folks so badly that you thought about hitting them or ruining their reputation or trying to hurt them somehow? What would someone have to do to make you want to go that far in responding to him or her?

JESUS UNDER A MICROSCOPE (MARK 1:12-15)

The first eleven verses of Mark are glowing: they show us a clear picture of Jesus as the Messiah who had come to save the Israelites. Prophecies had predicted his coming, and God himself came down to recognize him as his Son. It makes sense, then, that so many people fell at his feet and worshiped him. Given the nature of these first eleven verses, the plot twist that happens "immediately" in the next four verses may come as something of a shocker.

> [12]And the Spirit immediately drove him out into the wilderness. [13]He was in the wilderness forty days, tempted by Satan; and he was with the wild beasts; and the angels waited on him.
>
> [14]Now after John was arrested, Jesus came to Galilee, proclaiming the good news of God, [15]and saying, "The time is fulfilled, and the kingdom of God has come near; repent, and believe in the good news."

Verse 12

What do we know from earlier verses in Mark about this "Spirit"? Is the Spirit's action here surprising to you?

Verse 13

What happens out in the desert? Why do you think Mark included each of the details?

The word *Satan* means "adversary" or "enemy." Why do you think Jesus had an enemy?

Overall, how does this forty-day experience strike you? Is it something you'd sign up for? Why do you think the Spirit sent Jesus out for this experience? Why do you think Jesus went—and stayed?

Verses 14-15

How do you think the news of John's arrest affected Jesus? What did Jesus do after John was arrested? What was he proclaiming? What images does the phrase "kingdom of God" bring to your mind? What does the word *repent* mean?

Overview

How does the presence of an active "enemy" and the arrest of John affect the tone of this story? Does it still seem like the "gospel" of Jesus (that is, the announcement of victory)?

How does Jesus respond to the desert experience and the arrest?

JESUS THROUGH A TELESCOPE

The foreboding we get in this opening section of the text turns out to be pretty accurate. Jesus ends up having many enemies. Let's pull back a little bit and scan the four Gospels to see a broader picture of how this darker side of the story is played out.

The Pharisees went and plotted to entrap him in what he said. (Matthew 22:15)

They said this to test him, so that they might have some charge to bring against him. (John 8:6)

All in the synagogue were filled with rage. (Luke 4:28)

People were saying, "He has gone out of his mind." (Mark 3:21)

The crowd answered, "You have a demon!" (John 7:20)

The Jews answered him, "Are we not right in saying that you are a Samaritan and have a demon?" (John 8:48)

The Jews said to him, "Now we know that you have a demon." (John 8:52)

Many of them were saying, "He has a demon and is out of his mind." (John 10:20)

They were filled with fury and discussed with one another what they might do to Jesus. (Luke 6:11)

They got up, drove him out of the town, and led him to the brow of the hill on which their town was built, so that they might hurl him off the cliff. (Luke 4:29)

The Jews were seeking all the more to kill him. (John 5:18)

The Pharisees went out and immediately conspired with the Herodians against him, how to destroy him. (Mark 3:6)

They kept looking for a way to kill him. (Mark 11:18)

The Pharisees went out and conspired against him, how to destroy him. (Matthew 12:14)

The chief priests, the scribes, and the leaders of the people kept looking for a way to kill him. (Luke 19:47)

They wanted to arrest him. (Matthew 21:46)

They conspired to arrest Jesus by stealth and kill him. (Matthew 26:4)

Some began to spit on him, to blindfold him, and to strike him. (Mark 14:65)

They struck his head with a reed, spat upon him. (Mark 15:19)

After mocking him, they stripped him. (Mark 15:20)

They kept heaping many other insults on him. (Luke 22:65)

All of them said, "Let him be crucified!" (Matthew 27:22)

Those who passed by derided him, shaking their heads. (Matthew 27:39)

The soldiers also mocked him. (Luke 23:36)

The chief priests also, along with the scribes and elders, were mocking him. (Matthew 27:41)

The bandits who were crucified with him also taunted him. (Matthew 27:44)

SACRIFICIAL JESUS?

Looking back at the section in Mark and at all of these other verses, what are similarities you see? Differences?

What different people or groups are mentioned as Jesus' enemies? Why do you think so many people responded to Jesus in this way? What do we learn about Jesus from this?

Read the following quote and think about and discuss the questions that follow.

> Jesus was not a man to be distracted by the whims of others or persuaded by what was popular. His purpose and truth and life were propelled and determined by his Father. And there would be no deviating. This chorus of human spitting and hatred and outrage is a testament to Jesus' prophetic nature.
>
> He came as Light into a world that was fallen and dark. And those who live in darkness don't like lights so much—lights have a way of revealing. They have a way of chasing away lies and deceptions and false pride. Jesus was the Light and they hated him for it. They would have done anything to get rid of him. Their frantic attempts at destroying Jesus are a testament to the depth to which his razor-sharp message reached within them. . . .
>
> This chorus of negative responses highlights one more thing about Jesus—his utter, firm, persistent sacrificial nature. In his three years of ministry Jesus walked headlong toward death. At each awkward point of conflict with the Pharisees, at each run-in with his family, at each accusation

slapped across his face, he could have hesitated, deviated, adjusted the plan to soften the blow to himself.

During his flogging, he could have stopped everything, unleashed his Creator power and destroyed all around him. Each time he was spat upon, he could have called down floods from heaven to wipe away those who would spit in the face of Yahweh enfleshed. When taunted upon the cross, when laughed at, when derided for not being able to save himself, he *could* have called legions of angels to his rescue.

The fact that Jesus elicited ire and hatred and lashings and insults from those around him tells us something deep about his longing to embrace death on a cross for us. Where each blow would have left most of us reeling and running for our lives and comfort and control, Jesus faced it all. He never let up, he never smoothed things over to slow the onslaught of pain and torture and death. He marched steadily into it.

—from chapter eight, "They Struck His Head," in *God in the Flesh*

What do you think about the conclusions this quote draws about Jesus? Are these fair conclusions?

What are some possible reasons why people were so against Jesus' proclamation about "the good news of God"?

Of the two responses we've seen toward Jesus so far (worshiping him or striking him), which makes the most sense to you? Which is closer to your response to his message?

FURTHER EXPERIMENTS IN OPPOSITION

- Read Mark 14:32-50, where we read a detailed, intimate account of Jesus' temptation before his final, most brutal human pain. Do you think Jesus could have avoided his death on a cross? What does this section of Mark 14 reveal about why he ended up on a cross?

- Read chapter eight, "They Struck His Head," in *God in the Flesh*.

- Rent the movie *The Passion of the Christ,* starring Jim Caviezel as Jesus, and watch this portrayal of the suffering of Jesus' last few days. As you watch, be asking yourself the question "Why would he go through all this?"

3

They Left Their Nets

In this session we see Jesus call his first followers.

Jesus did that. He called people to follow him. And they were just regular folks, doing their regular lives. He asked them to drop everything and start following him. And do you know what? Some said yes. They left behind everything just to be with Jesus.

Have you ever set aside your own stuff so that you could be with someone? (Perhaps you skipped work or a class just to hang out with someone. Or maybe you passed up an opportunity to make a lot of money so you could be with someone you loved.) What's one of the biggest things you've ever seen anyone sacrifice to be with another person?

JESUS UNDER A MICROSCOPE (MARK 1:16-20)

After Mark gives us the overview of Jesus going into Galilee and proclaiming the good news of God, he gives us a close-up of Jesus interacting with people. Here we see fleshed out what it looked like for Jesus to announce his good news and call people to repent and believe in it.

[16]As Jesus passed along the Sea of Galilee, he saw Simon and his brother Andrew casting a net into the sea—for they were fishermen. [17]And Jesus said to them, "Follow me and I will make you fish for people." [18]And immediately they left their nets and followed him. [19]As he went a little farther, he saw James son of Zebedee and his brother John, who were in their boat mending the nets. [20]Immediately he called them; and they left their father Zebedee in the boat with the hired men, and followed him.

Verses 16-17

What's the life of a fisherman like? If you were Simon or Andrew, would you have any questions about Jesus' brief invitation? What would you ask him?

Verse 18

What would it mean for these men to leave their nets? How would it feel?

Verses 19-20

What's different this time around? What's similar between this story and the one in verses 16-18?

Overview

These are two brief stories. Why do you think Mark tells the stories this way? Notice what details are included and what details are not. Any ideas why that's the case?

Why do you think these fishermen left their nets and followed Jesus?

JESUS THROUGH A TELESCOPE

Simon, Andrew, James and John set aside the comfort and familiarity and security of their trade as fishermen. But these men weren't the only people to set aside dear things for Jesus. Consider a few other things that people set aside for Jesus, seemingly without flinching.

> *As Jesus was walking along, he saw a man called Matthew sitting at the tax booth; and he said to him, "Follow me." And he got up and followed him.* (Matthew 9:9)

> *A man was there named Zacchaeus; he was a chief tax collector and was rich. . . . When Jesus came to the place, he looked up and said to him, "Zacchaeus, hurry and come down; for I must stay at your house today." So he hurried down and was happy to welcome him. . . . Zacchaeus stood there and said to the Lord, "Look, half of my possessions, Lord, I will give to the poor; and if I have defrauded anyone of anything, I will pay back four times as much."* (Luke 19:2, 5-6, 8)

> *Mary took a pound of costly perfume made of pure nard, anointed Jesus' feet, and wiped them with her hair. The house was filled with the fragrance of the perfume.* (John 12:3)

> *A woman in the city, who was a sinner, having learned that he was eating in the Pharisee's house, brought an alabaster jar of ointment. She stood behind him at his feet, weeping, and began to bathe his feet with her tears and to dry them with her hair. Then she continued kissing his feet and anointing them with the ointment.* (Luke 7:37-38)

BEAUTIFUL JESUS?

Matthew was a tax collector. How would leaving his job be different from the fishermen leaving their jobs? How would it be similar?

Zacchaeus was also a tax collector. What all did he give up after just a brief encounter with Jesus? Given how corrupt tax collectors were at the time, how big was Zacchaeus's promise in terms of money? Why do you think he made such a huge commitment?

Women in Jesus' day were usually landless and often had no paying jobs. Costly nard encased in a jar was often their only capital (and it often served as their dowry). How are these women's acts of sacrifice similar to or different from the sacrifices of the men we've been considering?

Read the following quote and then consider the questions that follow.

Now, perhaps a better understanding of the cultural context would clear up some of these seemingly rash actions. Maybe Zebedee would be happy to see his sons go off with a rabbi. Perhaps Jesus had known these fishermen for quite some time and had gone over with them what a life of following him would look like. Maybe they were tired of fishing. Perhaps Matthew was a friend of Jesus' already. Perhaps wasting whole jars of nard was commonplace. Perhaps a bath of tears was normal in their culture. Perhaps.

But what is crystal clear in the Gospel telling of these stories is an undeniable sense of awe and epic abandonment. When Jesus is in the room, treasures and lives and careers have a way of getting flung away. Social customs and etiquette and decorum have a way of dissolving into nothing. This is the clear testimony of these verses.

There is a beauty in Jesus that calls forth reckless abandon.

Jesus is beautiful. And at a word from him, thick-bearded men with calloused, practiced hands drop their familiar nets. At merely seeing him from behind, a woman invites herself into a house she has no right to be in and halts a dinner party with her weeping. . . .

What was it in Jesus that elicited such epic abandonment? His holiness, his brilliant teachings, his palpable authority? Maybe it was his power or gentleness or divine scent? Or maybe, when you add up all these aspects, you get a striking, compelling, beautiful man. A man who calls forth to something deep within, with a call that makes all other calls or impulses or duties fade away.

Deep calls to deep. And human ambition and control and fear fell from human hands. Witness the beauty of this carpenter, and a long life of measured, careful steps might just get traded in for skipping along with him into the great unknown.

Jesus had this effect on people.

And he still does.

—from chapter ten, "They Left Their Nets," in *God in the Flesh*

What would it take for you to leave your job or possessions behind for someone? What questions would you ask before throwing away everything you've been working for?

Do you think the fishermen, tax collectors and two women asked questions first? In the end, why do you think they did it?

FURTHER EXPERIMENTS IN LEAVING NETS

• Read Mark 2:13-17, where we see what happened with the tax collector whom Jesus invited into his posse. Why do you think he throws a party? Why do you think the religious leaders are so upset? At the end of the party, do you think Matthew is still glad he decided to follow Jesus?

- Read chapter ten, "They Left Their Nets," in *God in the Flesh.*

- Read the parables of the treasure and the pearl (Matthew 13:44-46). How do these parables shed light on the actions of these fishermen in Mark? Do you think they "joyfully" left their occupations and families?

- If you know a Christian who left a lot to follow Jesus, or who still sacrifices a lot for Jesus, buy this person some coffee and ask why he or she did it. Or watch the 1986 documentary *Mother Teresa,* made by Ann and Jeanette Petrie. As you watch, listen for insights into why Mother Teresa set aside so much for Jesus.

4

They Became Silent

In session four we're going to begin considering Jesus' teaching by looking at the effect it had on people. You can tell a lot about teachers by looking at the faces in their classroom. And it turns out that Jesus' teaching made people's jaws drop!

When was the last time you were amazed by someone's teaching? Why were you amazed? If you haven't been amazed, have you ever been surprised or shocked or really caught by a talk or speech or class or set of lyrics?

JESUS UNDER A MICROSCOPE (MARK 1:21-22)

So far, this chapter has revealed Jesus' true nature as God's Son, the Messiah. We have seen that Jesus apparently is going to have some enemies as he proclaims his announcement of victory. This doesn't stop Jesus, though. He heads into the region of Galilee and proclaims this news. While walking along the sea, he calls four fishermen to follow him. (They do!) And the next thing we know . . .

²¹They went to Capernaum; and when the sabbath came, he

entered the synagogue and taught. ²²They were astounded
at his teaching, for he taught them as one having authority,
and not as the scribes.

Verse 21

What do you know about the Jewish sabbath and about what
goes on in a synagogue?

Verse 22

What did people think of Jesus' teaching? Why? How is Jesus'
teaching different from what they were used to? How might the
scribes have been teaching? What does "authority" mean to you?

JESUS THROUGH A TELESCOPE

This time in the Capernaum synagogue will not be the last time
Jesus teaches. Far from it. Jesus' good news is something he
teaches about a lot, and almost always there is an extreme reaction
to his teaching. Let's zoom past this first teaching experience and
get a more global view of how folks responded to his teaching.

*All who heard him were amazed at his understanding and his an-
swers. When his parents saw him they were astonished.* (Luke
2:47-48)

*Now when Jesus had finished saying these things, the crowds were
astounded at his teaching.* (Matthew 7:28)

*He came to his hometown and began to teach the people in their
synagogue, so that they were astounded and said, "Where did this
man get this wisdom?"* (Matthew 13:54)

When the crowd heard it, they were astounded at his teaching.
(Matthew 22:33)

They were astounded at his teaching, for he taught them as one having authority, and not as the scribes. (Mark 1:22)

They were all amazed, and they kept on asking one another, "What is this? A new teaching." (Mark 1:27)

On the sabbath he began to teach in the synagogue, and many who heard him were astounded. They said, "Where did this man get all this? What is this wisdom that has been given to him?" (Mark 6:2)

They were afraid of him, because the whole crowd was spellbound by his teaching. (Mark 11:18)

He began to teach in their synagogues and was praised by everyone. (Luke 4:15)

All spoke well of him and were amazed at the gracious words that came from his mouth. (Luke 4:22)

They were astounded at his teaching, because he spoke with authority. (Luke 4:32)

They were not able in the presence of the people to trap him by what he said; and being amazed by his answer, they became silent. (Luke 20:26)

About the middle of the festival Jesus went up into the temple and began to teach. The Jews were astonished at it, saying, "How does this man have such learning, when he has never been taught?" (John 7:14-15)

WISE JESUS?

What similarities do you see in Jesus' listeners? What differences come out in these verses? Can you imagine a teacher creating this kind of response today?

Why do you think people (friends and enemies alike) were so floored by Jesus' teaching? Read the following quote and consider the questions that follow.

These responses to Jesus tell us, with utter clarity and surety, that when Jesus taught, something amazing was taking place. Every time he opened his mouth, his brilliance and genius came out, simply and easily. . . .

John tells us that Jesus was the Word become flesh.

We considered in an earlier chapter, "Word" (or *logos* in Greek) means truth or reason or logic or reality. And John tells us that this ultimate expression of truth slipped skin on and became Jesus. So Jesus *was* truth. He *was* logic. He *was* reality.

Ultimately *logos* isn't about ideas. It's about reality—what is. And reality, of course, is the truest thing around. It defines truth. . . .

No wonder the people were stunned when he began to teach. No wonder it seemed like nothing they had ever heard before. No wonder they were silenced. . . .

The most cleverly laid theological trap came apart before Jesus. The most unfair, contrived, pointed question fell silent and limp at one word from Jesus. After a while his opponents stopped trying to debate him. With a simple story Jesus could unseat the proudest debaters of his day. With one image Jesus could name, with utter precision and efficiency, a truth of human existence that until that moment had seemed to all around him a tangled mess.

—from chapter five, "They Became Silent," in *God in the Flesh*

Based on the first twenty-two verses of Mark, how do you think Mark would explain the response Jesus gets to his teaching? Do you think Mark would be surprised by this response?

How familiar are you with Jesus' teachings? Do you find them amazing? Do you sense authority in his words?

FURTHER EXPERIMENTS IN BEING AMAZED

- Read Mark 6:1-6 to find out how Jesus' teaching went over in his hometown. Why do you think they respond as they do?

- Read the Sermon on the Mount (Matthew 5—7), which contains a large section of Jesus' teaching. How does it hit you? As you read through it, do you get a sense of what the crowd in the synagogue means by his "authority"?

- Read chapter five, "They Became Silent," in *God in the Flesh*.

5

They Fell Down Before Him

This is a weird session. Let's just be honest about that straight up. We'll be considering Jesus' authority by looking at a fight he gets into with a demon. Then we'll walk through the four Gospels looking at people who threw themselves at Jesus' feet. It's some pretty gut-oriented stuff. Not a lot of touchy-feely heart stuff or intellectual mind stuff. Jesus' authority—and folks' unmistakable response to it—plunges deep into the world of guts and human will.

Have you ever felt humbled before someone? Ever meet royalty or somebody famous and feel like you weren't worthy to be in their presence? Who's the most famous or most powerful person you've ever met?

JESUS UNDER A MICROSCOPE (MARK 1:23-28)

We're now twenty-two verses into Mark 1. When we last left Jesus, he had gone to the synagogue in Capernaum and taught. And everyone was freaking out about his teaching—amazed at his words and the authority of his teaching. It's in that context of a general buzz going through the crowd at the synagogue that we get plunged into our next six verses.

> [23]Just then there was in their synagogue a man with an unclean spirit, [24]and he cried out, "What have you to do with us, Jesus of Nazareth? Have you come to destroy us? I know who you are, the Holy One of God." [25]But Jesus rebuked him, saying, "Be silent, and come out of him!" [26]And the unclean spirit, convulsing him and crying with a loud voice, came out of him. [27]They were all amazed, and they kept on asking one another, "What is this? A new teaching—with authority! He commands even the unclean spirits, and they obey him." [28]At once his fame began to spread throughout the surrounding region of Galilee.

Verses 23-24
So who, exactly, is doing the talking here? What does it want from Jesus?

How does the evil spirit identify Jesus—what does it call him? Why do you think the demon says what it says?

Verses 25-26
What do we learn about Jesus by looking at his response to the evil spirit? What happens after Jesus speaks? Why?

Verses 27-28
How would you have responded if you were in the crowd? What is the overwhelming response?

Overview
What new things do we learn about Jesus in this section? What do we see here that confirms what Mark has already written about Jesus in the first twenty-two verses?

JESUS THROUGH A TELESCOPE

This evil spirit publicly acknowledges Jesus' authority by leaving when commanded to. And the crowd is left surprised by the authority Jesus seems to have. But it doesn't end there. For the next three years, people keep publicly acknowledging his obvious authority.

Suddenly a leader of the synagogue came in and knelt before him. (Matthew 9:18)

A [Syrophoenician] woman . . . came and bowed down at his feet. (Mark 7:25)

A man ran up and knelt before him. (Mark 10:17)

There was a man covered with leprosy. When he saw Jesus, he bowed with his face to the ground. (Luke 5:12)

When Mary came where Jesus was and saw him, she knelt at his feet. (John 11:32)

When Jesus said to [the detachment of soldiers and police of the high priest], "I am he," they stepped back and fell to the ground. (John 18:6)

On entering the house, [the wise men from the East] saw the child [Jesus] with Mary his mother; and they knelt down and paid him homage. (Matthew 2:11)

[The Samaritan] prostrated himself at Jesus' feet. (Luke 17:16)

Simon Peter . . . fell down at Jesus' knees, saying, "Go away from me, Lord, for I am a sinful man!" (Luke 5:8)

Whenever the unclean spirits saw him, they fell down before him and shouted, "You are the Son of God!" (Mark 3:11)

When [the demoniac] saw Jesus from a distance, he ran and bowed down before him. (Mark 5:6)

The woman, . . . in fear and trembling, fell down before him.
(Mark 5:33)

JESUS WITH AUTHORITY?

What different types of people fell at their knees before Jesus?

When have you been humbled around someone? What did it feel like? Consider the following quote and the few questions that are below it.

> This was the life of Jesus. His authority and rightful lordship emanated from him, and folks, from the demon-possessed to the powerful to the desperate, found themselves at his feet.
>
> Perhaps we could explain away the kneeling of mere outcasts and lepers. But rulers? Close friends? A group of soldiers on a serious mission? Foreign wise men? . . .
>
> There was something about Jesus, an authority that was as real and palpable as that dirt on his sandaled feet.
>
> These kneeling verses clarify for us that Jesus' place is on a throne. He has authority and lordship. He is a Lord. *The* Lord. He may be a merciful, graceful, patient, loving Lord, but let there be no mistake: he is Lord. Our place is at his feet. Humbled. Silent. He may woo people to him as a lover. But he doesn't have to. At his word he could command all attention and obedience. He is Lord over all. That is not just fodder for a worship song—that is reality.
>
> He is Lord over everything. His authority knows no bounds. It extends into every corner of our lives, every moment of our days, every decision we make.

—from chapter six, "They Fell Down Before Him," from *God in the Flesh*

In what contexts do we normally use the word *authority?* In those cases, where does the authority come from?

In the pages of the Gospels we see Jesus exercise authority over demons, illness, death, weather, wisdom and people. Where could that kind of authority come from?

FURTHER EXPERIMENTS IN FALLING AT HIS FEET

- Read Mark 4:35—5:20, where we see Jesus exercise authority over the sea and a chained-up possessed man. Look for similarities in the two scenes you encounter.

- Read chapter six, "They Fell Down Before Him," from *God in the Flesh.*

- Since humility and gut acknowledgment of authority are so rare these days, spend at least thirty minutes a day for the next week kneeling on the ground somewhere. Perhaps do it near some large natural place, such as a river or mountain, or even by just looking up at the sky. I know it's not the real thing, but what is it like to even "practice" humility through this simple, physical exercise?

6

They Brought to Him All the Sick

In this session we're going to examine one of the more interesting responses people had to Jesus—namely, carrying their friends to him. Literally. Everywhere Jesus went, people brought their needy friends to him. What does this tell us about these people and (more importantly) about Jesus himself? This type of response to Jesus was so common that we have to deal with it head-on.

What's one of the worst periods of illness or injury you've ever had? At that time, did many friends come around to help you out? Did you heal gradually or quickly?

JESUS UNDER A MICROSCOPE (MARK 1:29-34)

Jesus' life as Messiah and Son of God is starting to take a little more shape, now that we're twenty-eight verses into the book. It's quite a sabbath in the synagogue! Jesus teaches and everyone is floored by his teaching. Then there's the showdown between Jesus and an evil spirit, which Jesus wins hands down. And the crowd is amazed again, spreading news everywhere around Galilee about Jesus' authority. It's at this intense moment that we again pick up the action with Jesus and his four followers.

> [29]As soon as they left the synagogue, they entered the house of Simon and Andrew, with James and John. [30]Now Simon's mother-in-law was in bed with a fever, and they told him about her at once. [31]He came and took her by the hand and lifted her up. Then the fever left her, and she began to serve them.
>
> [32]That evening, at sundown, they brought to him all who were sick or possessed with demons. [33]And the whole city was gathered around the door. [34]And he cured many who were sick with various diseases, and cast out many demons; and he would not permit the demons to speak, because they knew him.

Verses 29-30
Why do you think Jesus' four followers told him about Simon's mother-in-law? Do you think they were expecting anything from Jesus other than sympathy?

Verse 31
How do you imagine this scene playing out? What do you make of the details Mark gives us (Jesus taking her hand, his helping her up, her beginning to wait on them and so on)? Do we learn anything about Jesus in this scene?

Verses 32-34
The Jewish sabbath ends at sunset. Once the sabbath ends, what happens? How many people does it sound like we're talking about here? What types of people are probably in the crowd?

Why do you think people brought the needy to Jesus? What did Jesus do?

Overview

What impression do you think folks had of Jesus that night? What adjective might they use to describe him?

JESUS THROUGH A TELESCOPE

That first night in Capernaum was quite a night. Everyone from the town of Capernaum had brought their needy, sick, hurting friends to Jesus. What a crowd! Well, word of Jesus' powerful touch was going to spread like wildfire. Let's push fast-forward and see how this kind of reaction plays out for the next three years.

They brought to him all the sick, those who were afflicted with various diseases and pains, demoniacs, epileptics, and paralytics. (Matthew 4:24)

That evening they brought to him many who were possessed with demons. (Matthew 8:16)

All in the crowd were trying to touch him, for power came out from him. (Luke 6:19)

After the people of that place recognized him, they sent word throughout the region and brought all who were sick to him. (Matthew 14:35)

People were bringing even infants to him that he might touch them. (Luke 18:15)

All who had diseases pressed upon him to touch him. (Mark 3:10)

She had heard about Jesus, and came up behind him in the crowd and touched his cloak, for she said, "If I but touch his clothes, I will be made well." (Mark 5:27-28)

Immediately the people recognized him, and ran about the whole neighborhood and began to bring sick people on their pallets to any place where they heard he was. (Mark 6:54-55 RSV)

Wherever he went, into villages or cities or farms, they laid the sick in the marketplaces, and begged him that they might touch even the fringe of his cloak. (Mark 6:56)

POWERFUL JESUS?

What similarities do you notice in these stories? How do you imagine these people conducting themselves as they brought their friends? Consider the quote and questions that follow.

First we need to recognize that not only did the sick seek him out unabashedly but also friends and relatives of the sick went out of their way to get their sick friends and this powerful Jesus together. The Gospels make it clear that upon word of Jesus' entrance into a town many folks would drop whatever they were doing, run to their diseased, oppressed friends and carry them around town, sweating, running, yelling out to anyone who would listen, "Where is he? Where is he? Is he still here?"

The Gospel records also make it clear that no attention was given to Jesus' schedule, no space was politely afforded him. There was no standing on the outskirts of the crowd politely waiting your turn, no quietly raised arms. Folks ran and pushed and scrambled and shoved—all for a touch. . . .

And who can blame them for their lack of politeness? Who can look down on them for acting so brashly and suddenly? What else could they do? To be around so much need and so much power—they just had to get the two together. There was no choice or deliberation. There was no calm bowing to social customs. They were in the presence of power! Power like none other they had ever experienced.

And what do you do when you see such power? You leap. You run. You get up off your couch because there's finally a place to take your own need and the needs of those dearest to you.

—from chapter nine, "They Brought to Him All the Sick," in *God in the Flesh*

So all these folks ran their friends to Jesus. But why was this recorded? Why do you think Mark gives us that part of the story?

Do you think that Jesus really healed all those people? If so, do you think healing is still possible today?

FURTHER EXPERIMENTS IN HEALING

- Read Mark 5:21-43, where Jesus has interesting encounters with a sick old woman who sneaks up to him, with a ruler of the synagogue who begs for help and with that ruler's dead little daughter. What new things do you learn about Jesus in this story?

- Read chapter nine, "They Brought to Him All the Sick," in *God in the Flesh*.

- Find a place in your hometown where a lot of needy people congregate. Spend some time there observing. Write down the "feel" of the place, the overwhelming emotion. Reread Mark 1:29-34 while sitting there and contemplate how Jesus might have influenced the people around you if they had been there in Capernaum.

- As an exercise in creatively entering the text, pretend you're Peter writing in your diary after that amazing night with Jesus and your entire hometown at your house. What would you record? What thoughts or feelings or questions would you write down?

7

They Were Seized by Amazement

Welcome to session seven, the land of the weird and shocking! In this session we're taking a look at how *unpredictable* Jesus was. Strange, in fact. If the word *holy* in part means "set apart, other, not like us," then Jesus was definitely a holy man. Seems that everywhere he went, folks were shocked by what he did and said. This guy definitely marched to the tune of a different drummer!

Have you ever been around someone who was surprising or shocking? When was the last time you were amazed by someone? What's the most shocking thing you've ever seen someone do?

JESUS UNDER A MICROSCOPE (MARK 1:35-39)

Before diving into the next five verses, it's important to remember where we are. Jesus begins his life of ministry by entering Galilee and proclaiming his good news to everyone. He calls four fishermen to leave everything and follow him—and they do. Then, starting in verse 21, the five of them go to Capernaum, the hometown of two of the fishermen, Simon and Andrew. What Simon and Andrew see next must have made their day—

Jesus teaches in the synagogue and everyone is stunned by his amazing teaching. Then he casts a demon out of a man in the synagogue.

I'm sure their heads were already spinning as they walked back to Simon's place. Then Jesus heals Simon's mother-in-law and, once the sabbath is officially over, the whole town (yes, the whole town!) comes to Simon's house to see if Jesus can heal their sick and needy friends. And he does. All night it's miracle after miracle at the door of Simon's house. The next morning Simon must have been stoked to see what would happen next.

> [35]In the morning, while it was still very dark, he got up and went out to a deserted place, and there he prayed. [36]And Simon and his companions hunted for him. [37]When they found him, they said to him, "Everyone is searching for you." [38]He answered, "Let us go on to the neighboring towns, so that I may proclaim the message there also; for that is what I came out to do." [39]And he went throughout Galilee, proclaiming the message in their synagogues and casting out demons.

Verse 35
How late does it sound like Jesus was up the night before? What time does he get up? What is he getting up for? What do you imagine those early morning hours might have been like for Jesus?

Verses 36-37
Why do you think "everyone is searching" for Jesus? Has the fervor and excitement died down from the night before?

Pretend you are Simon on that morning. You finally find Jesus and tell him how everyone is psyched to see him. What would you expect him to say or do?

Verses 38-39

What are the reasons Jesus gives for leaving Capernaum? What ends up happening in the other towns?

Overview

How is this scene similar and different from the other time we saw Jesus alone in the wilderness (Mark 1:12-13)? What happens right after both periods of being alone? If Jesus is "marching to the beat of a different drummer," who's beating that drum?

JESUS THROUGH A TELESCOPE

On this first Capernaum morning, Jesus surprised Simon and the crowd. He didn't do what they expected. Hopefully they got used to having slack jaws, because the surprises and gasps would continue for the next three years.

They were amazed, saying, "What sort of man is this?" (Matthew 8:27)

The crowds were amazed and said, "Never has anything like this been seen in Israel." (Matthew 9:33)

All the crowds were amazed. (Matthew 12:23)

They were greatly astounded. (Matthew 19:25)

They were all amazed and glorified God, saying, "We have never seen anything like this!" (Mark 2:12)

They were overcome with amazement. (Mark 5:42)

They were utterly astounded. (Mark 6:51)

They were greatly astounded. (Mark 10:26)

They were amazed, and those who followed were afraid. (Mark 10:32)

Pilate was amazed. (Mark 15:5)

Everyone was amazed at all that he was doing. (Luke 9:43)

Amazement seized all of them, and they glorified God and were filled with awe, saying, "We have seen strange things today." (Luke 5:26)

HOLY JESUS?

Which of the preceding quotes did you like the most? What's common in all of these verses? Give a few examples of what kinds of "strange things" it would take for you to be truly amazed today? Why do you think people were so amazed by Jesus?

What does it tell us about Jesus that so many people were amazed by him? Read the following passage out loud and then consider the questions that follow.

Given how cynical and dulled of senses we can be as a species, it's significant that Jesus caused shock everywhere he went. If we saw only a few shocked people in the Gospels, it would be nothing worthy of note. But what do you do with whole crowds that are shocked? What about multitudes standing with gaping jaws?

And don't you think it's remarkable that those who recorded these Gospels felt it was necessary to record this part of the story? This chorus of amazement must be significant. But what does it teach us about Jesus? . . .

[It certainly teaches us that] Jesus was strange and different and shocking. And [that] people couldn't help but stare. That is the story that the Gospels tell again and again. It is safe to say that, of all the things Jesus saw on human faces as he walked this earth, dropped jaws was one of them. It was as if one sustained gasp followed Jesus wherever he went. Never did what you thought he was going to do. Never said what you assumed he would say. Never sought out those you would have guessed. Never avoided those you assumed he would. He was a strange man, this carpenter.

—from chapter three, "They Were Seized by Amazement," in *God in the Flesh*

Based on what he's written so far, do you think Mark would be surprised that Jesus shocked so many people? Given what Mark has already made clear about Jesus, how might he explain all these gaping jaws and stunned looks?

If you had been in Capernaum, how might you have responded to Jesus? Do you think it's still possible to be surprised by Jesus?

FURTHER EXPERIMENTS IN BEING SHOCKED

- Read Mark 6:45-52, where we see Jesus not only surprise his followers but also scare the pee out of them! How do you suppose his followers' understanding of Jesus changed after this episode?

- Read chapter three, "They Were Seized by Amazement," in *God in the Flesh*.

- Look up a few of the small verses that describe people's shock and amazement. Read the full stories and find out what was so shocking in Jesus. In each of the cases you look up, try to imagine yourself there and think about how you would have felt. Would you have been shocked or amazed too?

- Read chapter five, "Profile: What I Would Have Noticed," from Philip Yancey's book *The Jesus I Never Knew*. Or read chapter two, "Jesus: God's Dirty Feet," from *Jesus with Dirty Feet*. What new things do you notice about the life and ways of Jesus?

8

He Touched Her Hand

This session is about Jesus' hands. Yeah, his hands.

Perhaps more than with any other religious figure ever, the story of Jesus' hands is observed and recorded in the books that tell the story of his life. And not only his hands but also his eyes and heart and guts. Jesus' internal life, his affection for people and his manner among them were things that all four Gospel writers felt it was important to record. Given the cost of papyrus (this wasn't the world of cheap paper and pens and endless chat rooms that we live in today), it is extraordinary that these details were recorded. It's something worthy of our attention.

Who's the most compassionate person you've ever met? Do you spend much time around needy people or people who are ill? What does it feel like to be around them?

JESUS UNDER A MICROSCOPE (MARK 1:40-45)

To the surprise of Simon, Jesus decided to head out and teach in other villages. And so he did. After the expansive, general verse "And he went throughout Galilee, proclaiming the message in their synagogues and casting out demons," the Mark text slows down and focuses in on one specific interaction Jesus had with a very unpopular man.

> [40]A leper came to him begging him, and kneeling he said to him, "If you choose, you can make me clean." [41]Moved with pity, Jesus stretched out his hand and touched him, and said to him, "I do choose. Be made clean!" [42]Immediately the leprosy left him, and he was made clean. [43]After sternly warning him he sent him away at once, [44]saying to him, "See that you say nothing to anyone; but go, show yourself to the priest, and offer for your cleansing what Moses commanded, as a testimony to them." [45]But he went out and began to proclaim it freely, and to spread the word, so that Jesus could no longer go into a town openly, but stayed out in the country; and people came to him from every quarter.

Verse 40

What do you think the emotional state of this man in verse 40 is like? What would it be like to be a leper? Why do you think he does what he does in the verse? What might the crowd have thought of his actions?

Verses 41-42

What do you think about Jesus' response? Do you think this compassionate gut response is how most people would respond to a leper?

Verses 43-44

What are some possible reasons for why Jesus sends this man away with the instructions that he does? Why do you think Jesus "sternly" warns the man?

Verse 45
So the guy disobeys! Can you blame him? Why do you think he went and told everyone what had happened? What resulted from his disobedience?

Overview
Most people treated lepers with fear, disdain and distance. How would you describe Jesus' treatment of the leper? Why do you think Mark slowed down and put in so many details about this encounter?

JESUS THROUGH A TELESCOPE

So Jesus felt compassion for the leper. And then touched him. Two responses that would have shocked the crowd. But it turns out this leper wouldn't be the last outcast Jesus would have deep affection for.

As we fast-forward through the Gospels, there are almost too many moments of affection and mercy and compassion to list. Let's walk through several to get a clearer picture of Jesus' manner among humans.

Moved with compassion, Jesus touched their eyes. (Matthew 20:34)

Moved with pity, Jesus stretched out his hand and touched him. (Mark 1:41)

He stretched out his hand and touched him. (Matthew 8:3)

He touched her hand. (Matthew 8:15)

He touched their eyes. (Matthew 9:29)

Jesus came and touched them, saying, "Get up and do not be afraid." (Matthew 17:7)

He took him aside in private, away from the crowd, and put his fingers into his ears, and he spat and touched his tongue. (Mark 7:33)

He took the blind man by the hand and led him out of the village. (Mark 8:23)

Jesus laid his hands on his eyes again. (Mark 8:25)

He came forward and touched the [coffin], and the bearers stood still. (Luke 7:14)

He touched [the soldier's] ear and healed him. (Luke 22:51)

When he saw the crowds, he had compassion for them, because they were harassed and helpless, like sheep without a shepherd. (Matthew 9:36)

When he went ashore, he saw a great crowd; and he had compassion for them. (Matthew 14:14)

As he came near and saw the city, he wept over it. (Luke 19:41)

Jesus began to weep. (John 11:35)

He was grieved at their hardness of heart. (Mark 3:5)

He was greatly disturbed in spirit and deeply moved. (John 11:33)

Jesus [was] again greatly disturbed. (John 11:38)

When the Lord saw [the widow], he had compassion for her and said to her, "Do not weep." (Luke 7:13)

Looking up to heaven, he sighed. (Mark 7:34)

He sighed deeply in his spirit. (Mark 8:12)

MERCIFUL JESUS?

Go back through these verses (and our section in Mark) and look for repeating words. What picture of Jesus emerges? What adjectives would you use to describe the Jesus portrayed here?

Read this description of Jesus:

Throughout the Gospels we are shown Jesus' hands as he touches the hurting, as he calms the fearful, as he holds someone's hand gently. This God, the Creator of all, this incarnate Word who could have spoken everything out of existence with one commanding word, this immense, looming Jesus softly held the hand of a blind man. Touched the ears of the deaf. Touched the wasting skin of lepers. Felt the eyes of the blind with his fingers. . . .

Instead of setting a blistering pace as a religious reformer, Jesus slowed down to talk with the poor. He could have healed long-distance all the time (it obviously was not hard for him, since he did it on several occasions), but instead of waving his hand over an entire village and creating mass healing, he walked slowly into the heart of a place, stopping to touch the sick. To hold hands. To embrace small babies as their proud mothers looked on. . . .

In the pages of the Gospels we are not only shown Jesus' hands. We are also shown his tears. His heart. The deep places of his spirit. It is meaningful that these seemingly insignificant details were recorded. The Gospel writers felt it important not only to quote Jesus but also to record what he was like. He sighed. His eyes softened with compassion. He grieved. He wept. He was disturbed. . . .

It is important that Jesus' great mercy and compassion are a part of the record of Scripture. . . . It changes everything to look at the flesh of God and see such mercy and tenderness and compassion.

—from chapter seven, "He Touched Her Hand," in *God in the Flesh*

What does it do to our perceptions of Jesus to see him sighing? Crying? Weeping? Tenderly touching a leper? Do you like this Jesus who is described in the pages of the Gospels? Why do you think this side of Jesus is so rarely talked about?

Jesus once said, "Come to me, all you that are weary and are carrying heavy burdens, and I will give you rest. Take my yoke upon you, and learn from me; for I am gentle and humble in heart, and you will find rest for your souls" (Matthew 11:28-29). Do you think that is a message that holds any relevance or appeal these days? How does that invitation sound to you?

FURTHER EXPERIMENTS IN COMPASSION

- Read and think through Mark 7:31-37, where we see another healing in which Jesus does some really weird things with his hands. As you study the encounter, think through why Jesus might have done the different weird things he did during the healing. How might Jesus' actions have been helpful to the man he was healing?

- Read chapter seven, "He Touched Her Hand," in *God in the Flesh*.

- Choose one of the verses from the long list in this chapter. Look up the context and read through the whole story, trying to picture it happening. Maybe draw a picture of the scene, trying to capture the emotion on Jesus' face, the sigh coming from his soul, the tears coming from his eyes! Or write a poem about the scene that helps get at Jesus' compassion.

- If you haven't already done so, watch the 1986 documentary *Mother Teresa* made by Ann and Jeanette Petrie. How powerful can compassion and mercy be these days? Do you see any aspects of Jesus reflected in Mother Teresa?

Further Resources

I hope these sessions have helped answer some of your questions about Jesus. He was quite a man, wasn't he?

The more I study about him, the more flesh I get on my picture of him. And the more I like him. He's not like I had always assumed. My pictures of him have always been so boring and flat and emotionless.

But he's so alive and unpredictable and tender and . . . *weird* sometimes! I like that. I think I would have liked to meet him back then. To sit with him and spend an afternoon together. Maybe just follow him around for a couple days and see people freak out or fall at his feet or spit at him.

Some say you still *can* meet with him. Jesus himself taught about how he was going to send his Spirit to those who want to follow him.

Maybe it *is* still possible to meet this man. Talk with a Christian friend or visit a local church to find out more about this.

If you find yourself wanting to know more about what it would have been to like to meet Jesus (but mingling with his Spirit doesn't sound attractive or possible), feel free to read the whole book of Mark. It's not long, and if just one chapter in it is helpful in clarifying what Jesus was really like, then the whole book couldn't hurt. There are sixteen chapters altogether. Not a bad little read.

You could also check out one of these other books:

Bruce, F. F. *The New Testament Documents: Are They Reliable?* 6th ed. Downers Grove, Ill.: InterVarsity Press, 2003.

Wondering if Mark is a reliable source of information about Jesus? This book's for those who have serious questions about the Bible and its trustworthiness.

Everts, Don. *God in the Flesh: What Speechless Lawyers, Kneeling Soldiers and Shocked Crowds Teach Us About Jesus.* Downers Grove, Ill.: InterVarsity Press, 2005.

This book came out of my fascination with what it would have been like to meet Jesus. I examine the different ways people responded to Jesus and what that tells us about the man himself.

Everts, Don. *Jesus with Dirty Feet: A Down-to-Earth Look at Christianity for the Curious and Skeptical.* Downers Grove, Ill.: InterVarsity Press, 1999.

This was the first book I wrote about Jesus and this Christianity thing he began. It's short, in a poetry-like form, and was powerful in helping me see Jesus without all the stereotypes that have accumulated around him and Christianity. If you haven't read it, it might be worth the two hours it takes to read through the whole thing. A quick, easy read that explodes many of the reigning myths about Jesus and Christianity.

Knechtle, Cliff. *Help Me Believe: Direct Answers to Real Questions.* Downers Grove, Ill.: InterVarsity Press, 2000.

With chapters that center on specific questions that folks have about Christianity, Jesus and the Bible, this is a great resource for looking up one man's take on the answers to questions you might have. Knechtle is never trite or flippant, and he takes each question seriously.

Lewis, C. S. *Mere Christianity.* Rev. ed. San Francisco: HarperSanFrancisco, 2001.

This one's short but so loaded that it will leave your mind satisfied. Lewis brings a scholar's precision and an Englishman's wit to bear upon this thing called Christianity. This book is unparalleled in its simple yet elegant exploration of the Christian faith.

McDowell, Josh. *More Than a Carpenter.* Wheaton, Ill.: Tyndale, 1977.

This is another quick read. If you have some questions about who Jesus was and what kind of evidence exists to support Christian claims about his divinity, crucifixion and so on, this might be the book for you.

Strobel, Lee. *The Case for Christ: A Journalist Investigates the Evidence for the Resurrection.* Grand Rapids: Zondervan, 2003.

This is a great read for those who still have many pressing questions about the Christian claims about Jesus. Strobel has the keen eyes of a journalist and uses them to examine the person of Jesus.

Happy hunting!

Leader's Guide

If you're planning on leading a group of people through some of these discussions, I think you're in for a treat. Not because this discussion guide is so cool but because Jesus is so cool. Whether looking at Jesus under a microscope by looking intently at one section of a Gospel or looking at him through a telescope by considering greater themes that recur throughout the Gospels, you're looking at Jesus.

And he's just a lot of fun to look at! He is intense and beautiful and strong and gentle and witty. He defies all our categories. Looking at him is always a good move.

And so is helping others look at him. Inviting other people to consider Jesus and look at his personality and manner and life is bound to be a lot of fun and quite fruitful.

Most of the discussion sessions are self-explanatory for those going through them. But I'll touch briefly on some helpful things to think about as someone leading others through the sessions.

1. GATHER YOUR FRIENDS

As you think about folks in your life, are there any who you think could really benefit from looking at Jesus? If so, invite them! Just ask them if they'd like to put an ancient Greek text under a microscope with you. Or something like that.

Be up-front about the point of these sessions—finding out what it would have been like to meet Jesus. If folks are interested in finding out, set a time and place to meet where you know you could have about an hour uninterrupted to go through the session.

2. MAKE YOUR PLAN

Thinking about who's coming will help you make a plan for which discussion to have with them. As you scan through the eight sessions, think about which aspect of Jesus might be most interesting to the folks coming. (The session notes that follow provide a quick overview of each discussion.) Ask yourself if there's a session or two that you feel would be most important for your friends to talk through.

Or do you want to invite them to walk through all of Mark 1 with you? For some people, considering a whole text like that will be most helpful. If eight sessions seems like too many, maybe start by asking them to do the first three with you, and then afterward they can decide whether or not they want to finish the chapter.

3. DO YOUR HOMEWORK

Once you have a plan, it'll be important to read through the text and the discussion questions to make sure you have a good handle on where the discussion might go. I suggest a three-step preparation process:

a. Begin by spending at least thirty minutes by yourself reading the text and marking it up with your thoughts and questions. Thirty minutes may seem like too much, but if you feel "done" after reading the text for ten minutes, press back into the text, asking new questions of it, examining individual words, trying to see it all through the eyes of those you'll be leading through it. Look up any confusing references, highlight repeating words, write down every potential question about the text that you can think of. Trust me, if you cheat on these thirty minutes, you will regret it later. You're going to want to know the section backwards and forwards.

b. Next, read through the questions and exercises we've listed in the session. I'm not assuming you'll use them all or find them all helpful. As you read through the discussion questions, mark the ones you like and want to use. Also, write in others you think will be important.

c. At the end of this leader's guide you will find even more help. I've provided session-by-session notes that include textual points that might be helpful and also some potential follow-up questions that might be useful in helping the discussion along at certain points. Read through these notes, marking the textual points and follow-up questions you think you'll use during the discussion.

If you have unanswered questions about the text, keep studying it and maybe ask a friend or two what they think about it. Don't feel like you have to have it all figured out. Just knowing the land you're about to lead your friends into can really help.

If at the end you want to invite your friends to do one of the "further experiments" with you, make a plan for which one you want to pursue and how you might go about it. Some of them could be done right after your discussion if you've planned ahead of time and have everything you need.

4. HAVE YOUR DISCUSSION

Remember, the point is looking at Jesus and talking about what you see. That's it. I think you might find the four exercises helpful in accomplishing that goal, so let me outline what the point of each exercise is.

Opening questions. I've started each session with a paragraph that gives an overview of the session. I think it could be helpful to have someone read this out loud to give everyone a road map. Then there are a couple of questions to help everyone begin to think about the topic. Asking one or two opening questions is also helpful in getting people to actually move their mouths (breaking the "sound barrier" is a key thing in any discussion group) and in helping the group get comfortable with each other. If there's a different question you'd like to use, feel free.

Jesus under a microscope. This is focused study time. If this is your first time together, you might want to outline some of what I go over in the introduction as a rationale for beginning by focusing in on one section. Encourage folks to stay "microscoped in" on this one section without trying to refer to a lot of other sources or stories about Jesus.

Once the ground rules are set, give folks a good ten minutes or so to "actively read" the text (for more on active reading, see the introduction). Then start walking through the text together, verse by verse. Feel free to use some of the notes and questions I've provided. Feel free to ignore some of them. Realistically, you won't have time to answer every question. Keep track of how much time you have and move the group along to further verses appropriately. Make sure you leave time for the overview questions as well.

Jesus through a telescope. This is where you allow your group to pull back from the text and consider a broader panorama of verses about Jesus. Read out loud the opening paragraph that introduces the list of verses and then give folks some more time to read through them and think through them. (If you think your group will explode if they get more quiet personal time to study, you might want to have the verses read out loud instead and then jump right into discussing them.)

What kind of Jesus? This third section could be how you close the discussion. The idea here is to take the up-close scene from Mark and put it together with the panorama from all the Gospels to come to some clearer understanding of what Jesus was like. I've provided some questions that may help the group process what they've studied. The point here is to help people be thoughtful about what they've seen.

You'll also find a quote from my book *God in the Flesh.* I've included this so that the group can have someone else's opinion to respond to. Since I most likely won't be in your group with you, it gives your friends the freedom to disagree or just honestly respond to what's there. This kind of dialogue can really help people further their own thinking.

The follow-up questions I've suggested at the end may help people not just look at Jesus but actually begin to interact with him a bit. You'll be the best judge about what will be most helpful for your group as a closing question or exercise.

Further experiments. Some of the folks in your group may not be done when everyone else is. The discussion may really intrigue them or confuse them. If that's the case, you'll want to provide some way to keep exploring or experimenting with the topic. I've provided some exercises to choose from. Or you can make up your own.

How do you know if people are "done" or want to explore more? You could tell the group that you are going to do one of the "further experiments" and see if anyone wants to do it with you. Their response will tell you a lot (though certainly not everything).

5. ENJOY YOURSELF!

Odds are, you're going to end up having a blast leading these discussions. I'm not saying there won't be tensions or arguments or confusion or interruptions or anything—there probably will be. I'm just saying that looking at Jesus is a great thing to be about. And you'll most likely have a great time.

There are some things we can do as leaders of discussion groups to "spoil" the fun, though. And that's no good. Many of us are getting much better at avoiding the more common ways of spoiling the discussion (using Christian language that doesn't make sense to anyone, speaking in clichés, acting as if there's a specific "right" answer to every question you ask and so on). But there are other ways I've seen discussions sabotaged as well. So I thought I'd highlight some of these other ways to spoil a perfectly good discussion so that we can try to avoid them as well.

Don't participate. This is a classic way to sabotage your discussion group right out of the gates. If you as the leader aren't involved in looking at Jesus yourself, if you aren't open to seeing new things, if you aren't honestly wrestling with the text or getting dizzied by the panorama of verses, then you'll make everyone feel awkward and uninspired.

On the other hand, if you are eager to see things in Jesus that you haven't before, if you're willing to ask good questions and actively read the text, you'll provide the spark for a group to really get involved and have a lively discussion.

Get caught up in being the leader. A nice way to make a discussion group painful is to use a different voice and/or persona than you usually do. You are the *leader*, after all. Shouldn't you be sitting up straight and bringing the whole deal some dignity by reading the questions really well and pronouncing all the Jewish names in the text perfectly? Another nice variation on this is being so awkward about leading that you are afraid to say anything and the group wanders aimlessly, never really getting to the text.

On the other hand, you could accept your role as leader and (here's an idea!) just be yourself as you lead. All groups need to be led, even informal groups. So be willing to do that. But don't let it keep you from being yourself. Some of the awkwardness will wear away in time, the more you get used to leading.

Stomp out silence. Silence is a golden, rare thing these days. It provides space for thought and reflection and allows one's heart and mind and soul time to mingle with each other. So if you're wanting to spoil the fun of actually learning and being changed by a discussion group, then by all means stomp out silence! Answering your own question or moving on quickly to the next question are two great ways of dealing with silence.

On the other hand, you could just get used to silence (just acknowledge that a second of silence feels like a minute of silence to the person leading the group) and allow people to mull over what's being talked about. When you feel the urge to jump in and break up the silence, just hold your tongue. You may be surprised by what comes out of someone else's mouth if you give them the time to get it out.

Be really defensive. Since the point of your group is to look at Jesus and learn more about him, a nice diversionary tactic is to get your group looking at you and your own thoughts and ideas. One way to do this is to get defensive when folks aren't seeing in Jesus exactly what you see or when they are doubting the veracity of what is in the text. Jump to the defense of the text and spew a couple of nice religious phrases (a stern, somewhat angry voice helps here) and you'll get your group ignoring Jesus and looking at you and your ideas in no time at all.

Or you could relax. You could realize that looking at Jesus is the point. You could admit in humility that you can't make anyone believe anything at all about Jesus. You can acknowledge that Scripture is what it is and let people wrestle with it as it sits there. You can allow people to doubt Scripture and be angry at Christianity and be suspect of Christians. You can rest in the peace that, in the end, it is only what people think of Jesus that matters, not what they think of Christians or Scripture or the Crusades or even you. And knowing this, you can relax and recognize that allowing people a chance to catch a glimpse of him is one of the most beautiful things you can do.

In the end I think you'll find that reading through Mark 1 is intense and beautiful and thrilling. Get ready to be encouraged and excited and humbled.

And thanks for being willing to lead other people into that experience as well.

SESSION NOTES

As you prepare each session, you will likely run into some textual questions. You might also wonder how to guide the discussion further at certain points. I provide these session notes to help you with both of these potential needs.

1. THEY WORSHIPED HIM

Purpose: This session is designed to confront head-on the question of Jesus' identity. Was he the Messiah? Was he divine?

Overview: The session begins with a study of Mark 1:1-11. These introductory verses are laden with claims about Jesus' identity. In

"Jesus Through a Telescope" we look at how common it was for people to worship Jesus. The session ends with a quote and set of questions designed to help people wrestle with the issue of Jesus' identity.

Textual notes and follow-up questions: Most of the discussion questions within the session are self-explanatory. Here I am including some textual notes that might be helpful to consider (and even point out to the group, if necessary) and some potential follow-up questions to take the conversation further at certain points.

Verse 1. *Gospel* is a Greek word that in Jesus' day meant "a message of good news." For example, after a victorious battle the Roman armies would send back to the emperor a runner who would bring the "gospel" of the war—the good news that they had won. What is the significance of using the word *gospel* here in reference to Jesus? Why do you think the author decided to call it the "beginning" of the gospel?

Christ is the Greek word for Messiah—the Savior for whom the hurting Israelites had been waiting for centuries. What does using the title Christ and the phrase "Son of God" to describe Jesus tell us about the author's opinion of Jesus?

Verses 2-3. These verses contain a quote from ancient Jewish prophecy—check out Isaiah 40:3 and Malachi 3:1. These were considered messianic prophecies, telling about the time when the Messiah would come. The Israelites knew the messianic prophecies well—they had been waiting for generations for this Messiah to come and save them. In this section quoted here God is telling the Israelites what to expect when the Messiah comes, including a messenger who would precede the Messiah.

Verses 4-6. Baptism is like a washing in water. So, what's a "baptism of repentance"? What would it look like for folks to "confess their sins"? Why would people do that? How many people responded to John's baptism? Putting all these details together, what do you think was going on out there in the desert?

Verses 9-11. What might it look like for "the heavens to be torn apart"? What adjectives or descriptors come up for you when you imagine something descending "like a dove"? How do you imagine the voice sounding to Jesus? What does this heavenly voice want to say?

Overview. In this section we find out what Mark, John the Baptist and God think about Jesus. What are their conclusions about Jesus, and how do they fit together?

Jesus Through a Telescope. Do these texts give the sense that this worship is a thought-out, dutiful response or just something that comes out of people? Give some examples from the texts.

If you had been there in the streets when all these folks stopped and worshiped Jesus, what might you have thought about them? How would you have responded to them?

2. THEY STRUCK HIS HEAD

Purpose: This session is designed to confront the fact that Jesus had enemies and had a purpose that drove him on despite all that his enemies did to him.

Overview: We begin with a surprising twist in the Mark 1 story: After blessing and honoring Jesus, the Spirit forces him into the desert, where he is tempted by Satan. Then we're told that John is arrested. Despite how seemingly dark these turns in the story are, we see Jesus begin to proclaim his message. This session then considers how much opposition Jesus faced throughout his life and ends by asking the question, why would Jesus keep walking into such torture? By looking at Jesus' enemies, we come to a deeper understanding of how important, and how driving, his purpose really was.

Verse 13. We know from the other Gospels that Jesus did not eat during these forty days. Why do you think he went without food for so long? (Reading about leaders from Israel's past who fasted for forty days might help shed some light in this practice. Try Exodus 24:18 and 34:28 to read about Moses or 1 Kings 19:8 to read about Elijah.)

Does the fact that Jesus has an enemy come as a surprise, given the beginning of the book? What is his enemy doing to him? Why do you think the details about the animals and angels are included?

Verses 14-15. Given the connection between John and Jesus, what does John's arrest signal to us as the readers? What might this arrest mean to Jesus as the one coming after John?

Galilee is a backwater region of Israel, simple fishing villages surrounding the Sea of Galilee. Jesus' hometown (Nazareth) isn't far from this area. Why might Jesus have started there?

There are two words in Greek for "time": *chronos* and *kairos*. *Chronos* is more general and literal, similar to when we would casually ask, "Hey, what *time* is it?" *Kairos* is more specific; it means "specially appointed time," similar to how we would say, "*The time* has come." Here in verse 15 it's *kairos*. What appointed time is Jesus talking about?

Is this "kingdom of God" a geographic thing? If not, what is it? What do you need in order to have a kingdom? What might it mean that the kingdom is "near"?

Overview. Does Jesus seem slowed down or cautious at all? Why do you think Jesus moves ahead so confidently, given the dangers that we now see in the story?

Sacrificial Jesus. What does it say about Jesus that so many people are arrayed against him and have such hatred and anger for him?

Is "repent and believe" an easy call to respond to? How was John's baptism of repentance preparing the way for Jesus' message? It turns out that not everyone liked his message. Why do you think that was the case, when it comes right down to it?

Pretend you can get into Jesus' head and heart. Why do you think he kept going despite the enemies he faced and the blows he was going to take? What other reasons for pressing on (other than those espoused in the quote) can you think of?

3. THEY LEFT THEIR NETS

Purpose: This session is designed to highlight the lordship of Jesus and the immense beauty and cost of following him.

Overview: First, this session takes a look at Jesus calling the four fishermen to leave their nets and follow him. Next, we consider the costs paid by two more men and two women (one man also leaves his job, and the other commits to give away vast sums of money; the two women sacrifice their costly jars of nard on Jesus). We end by contemplating why people would give up so much to follow Jesus.

Verses 16-17. Describe what life might have been like for Simon and Andrew. From start to finish, walk through what a day in their lives could have looked like.

Verse 18. Why do you think the men left their nets to follow Jesus? Why do you think Mark doesn't give us any dialogue from Simon and Andrew? How does their quick response (conspicuously devoid of any visible process on their part) make you feel?

Overview. As you look back over the fifteen verses that precede these stories, are there any clues as to why these guys respond so quickly to Jesus' call? What do we learn about Jesus in these first fifteen verses that causes these interactions to make more sense?

4. THEY BECAME SILENT

Purpose: This session is designed to illustrate how taken aback people were by Jesus' simple words and teachings.

Overview: First, we study the section of text where Jesus goes into the synagogue and teaches. It's a short section, but thinking about the crowd's response and then going on to read the long list of verses that show everyone's surprise and amazement at his teachings from throughout the Gospels is a striking study. This session ends by asking some serious questions about why everyone was so amazed at the words Jesus spoke.

Verse 21. Capernaum is Simon and Andrew's hometown. Why do you think they go there?

At the synagogue, Scripture would be read and then a Jewish man from the crowd would stand up and teach on it. Would there be anything weird about Jesus doing this?

Verse 22. In what contexts do we usually use the word *authority* today? Have you ever experienced someone with authority? How were the people used to being taught?

Wise Jesus? In the Luke 20 passage the "they" mentioned is actually a gaggle of professional lawyers. They were trained in the clever use of words and yet (as unbelievable as this is for a bunch of lawyers facing a mere carpenter) they became silent. Can you imagine this happening today?

5. THEY FELL DOWN BEFORE HIM

Purpose: This session explores Jesus' authority and how people in his own day acknowledged that authority in stark ways.

Overview: We begin in the synagogue with Jesus. Jesus finishes teaching and then a demon-possessed man cries out at Jesus and Jesus ends up rebuking the demon and casting him out of the man. We watch the crowd stand around dumbfounded, contemplating the authority Jesus just showed. Then we fast-forward through the Gospels, looking at different ways people acknowledged his authority (lots of kneeling) and end by asking questions about authority as a concept and about the authority Jesus seemed to have.

Verses 23-24. If you were filming this scene in the synagogue, how would you film it? (What kind of background music would you want? Who would you get close-ups of? How would the demon's voice sound?)

What "us" do you think the demon is referring to? Mark doesn't tell us what Jesus had taught in the synagogue, and yet he bothers to record the words of this evil spirit. Why do you think he quotes the evil spirit?

Verses 27-28. So, what is authority? How does this story help us more fully define "authority"? What news of Jesus' "fame" do you think was spreading around the region?

Jesus with Authority? Have you ever been on your knees or in the dirt at someone's feet before? Try it right now and see what it feels like. (No, really. Try it with someone you're with. It's in the name of philosophical inquiry—try it!) So, what did it feel like? Do you like being at someone's feet? Can you imagine any circumstance that would have you at someone's feet for real?

6. THEY BROUGHT TO HIM ALL THE SICK

Purpose: In this session we consider the power that Jesus had by looking at how many people sought out his healing touch for themselves and their sick friends.

Overview: We begin by leaving the synagogue. After amazing everyone at the synagogue with his teaching and authority over demons, Jesus and his friends go back to Simon's house. We begin this session by studying what happens at the house: Jesus heals Simon's mother-in-law and then ends up spending the whole night healing everyone from around the town. After spending some time at Simon's house, we zoom forward, taking in many of the accounts of folks streaming out to Jesus for healing. We end this session by considering why so many people flocked to Jesus for healing and what that teaches us about Jesus' power.

Verses 29-30. Does it seem to you that Mark slows down this chapter to tell us what the disciples told Jesus? If so, why do you think he does that?

Verses 32-34. What kind of "feel" or "buzz" do you think was in the air?

How late do you think this went? What kind of mood do you think there was in the crowd?

Overview. What was it that made people rush out of their homes right after sabbath to find Jesus?

Jesus Through a Telescope. What details in the verses give us some insight into the crowd's mood or motivation or nature?

Powerful Jesus? What does Jesus' healing power clarify for us about the "gospel," the great announcement of victory that Jesus came with?

If Jesus walked into your town, would you want to touch him? If you really believed he had healing power, who would you pick up and carry to him first?

Do you think anyone would pick you up?

7. THEY WERE SEIZED BY AMAZEMENT

Purpose: This session breaks through all of the "Jesus is so boring" stereotypes by looking at how surprising, and how "holy," Jesus really was.

Overview: We start with the morning after. Everyone wakes up after a night of miracles (the whole town had been at Simon's front door late into the night) and can't find Jesus. We look at the town's expectations (Where's our new favorite carpenter?) and at Jesus' shocking response (Sorry, I'm leaving now). From there we take a more global look at how many people Jesus surprised while walking around Israel for three years. We'll end by trying to make sense of all the amazement and shock: Why was everyone so surprised by Jesus? I thought he was boring!

Verse 35. What do you think it means for Jesus (the Messiah and Son of God, remember) to pray?

Looking back over all of Mark 1 up until now, are there any clues as to why Jesus might be doing this? Do his actions make sense with what we've read about him so far?

Verses 36-37. If you were Simon, what would be some of your first thoughts or instincts when you eventually got up that morning, given what happened the day before and the night before?

Verses 38-39. Still pretending you're Simon, what might you think of Jesus' response? Is it what you would have assumed he would say?

Why couldn't Jesus accomplish those things by staying put and letting everyone hear about him and come to him in Capernaum?

Overview. How does what happens after the sun comes up (Simon's hopes, the crowd's expectations, their agenda for Jesus) make more sense of what happens before the sun comes up (Jesus finding a lonely place to pray and seek his agenda)?

8. HE TOUCHED HER HAND

Purpose: This session confronts popular images of a harsh Jesus with the many details recorded in the Gospels that show his deep, personal compassion for those around him.

Overview: We begin the session by considering Jesus' healing of a leper (by touching him) and what that tells us about Jesus. We then read through a huge list of emotional, personal details about Jesus that are recorded in the Gospels. All these details underscore just how compassionate Jesus was. We end by asking some questions about Jesus' compassion and affection for people and what these examples do to our popular perceptions of him.

Verse 40. Leprosy was, and still is, a terrible disease. It caused gross disfiguration (skin decayed and started falling off in chunks), and those who had the disease literally became outcasts. They had to live outside regular cities in leper colonies, and whenever they came into town, they had to yell out, "Unclean!" in a loud voice so people would have fair warning about who was coming down the road.

Verses 41-42. The Greek word translated "pity" comes from the word for "gut." Having compassion means being moved in your guts, in essence. Why do you think Mark includes each detail in these verses (such as Jesus being filled with pity, reaching out his hand, touching, saying, "I do choose")?

Verses 43-44. Moses had given commandments for priests to ritually cleanse those who had been healed of a disease as a way of publicly welcoming them back into the mainstream of society (Leviticus 14). Why would Jesus order this man to do that?

Verse 45. How does this affect Jesus' plan to "go on to the neighboring towns" that he proclaimed to Simon in verse 38? How does that shed light on Jesus' warning to the guy to not tell anyone?

Overview. What might the people watching from the crowd have thought about Jesus' treatment of the leper?

Merciful Jesus? How do you reconcile this part of Jesus with other, more famous aspects of Jesus (such as his sacrificial death on a cross, his proclamations of truth, his claims to be the only way to God)?